The Perfect Gift
of Quiet Celebration

Thank You

This is a STAR FIRE book

STAR FIRE BOOKS
Crabtree Hall, Crabtree Lane
Fulham, London SW6 6TY
United Kingdom

www.star-fire.co.uk

First published 2007

07 09 11 10 08

1 3 5 7 9 10 8 6 4 2

Star Fire is part of The Foundry Creative Media Company Limited

The CIP record for this book is available from the British Library.

ISBN: 978 1 84451 946 0

Printed in China

Thanks to: Chelsea Edwards, Cat Emslie, Victoria Lyle,
Sara Robson, Gemma Walters and Nick Wells

The Perfect Gift
of Quiet Celebration

Thank You

Daisy Seal

Thank You

Foreword

I sit here in my beautiful cottage garden,
surrounded by grazing animals, birds in song and
the heady aroma of gorgeous flowers in full
bloom. Of course, such a wonderful, intoxicating
concoction has offered the inspiration for this
series of books which reflect on the values
underlying the best of our relationships:
generosity of spirit, kindness and love.

Daisy Seal

*Your kindness has brought
me many hours of peace
and happiness.*

*It's always worth a little effort
to show your appreciation.*

Yesterday I thought of you.
You popped into my mind,
like a sunrise warming the
sleep from my eyes.

There are times when we should bask in the glow of gratitude. Your time is now.

Sometimes we like to
remember another's help
with quiet sophistication.

On occasion, one should feel able to say thank you very loudly!

Your care has brought my inner garden out of winter, into the full flurry and dizziness of Spring.

A blizzard of colour and shape will greet you and bring joy every day.

It is often the quiet,
modest assistance that is
the most effective.

*You have never asked for thanks,
so you deserve them even more.*

Sometimes, just a simple thank you will do.

Greeting you today is a different person, thanks mostly, to you.

When I saw these, I thought of
you, giving me strength and
purpose in my hours of need.

We all need friends prepared
to remember us when we
were ourselves, not just
at our worst.

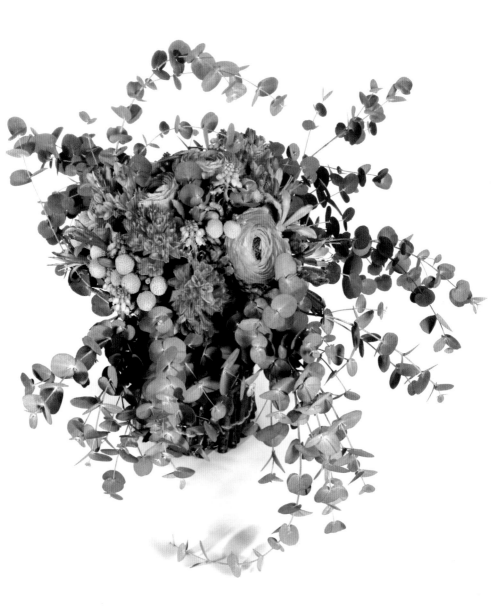

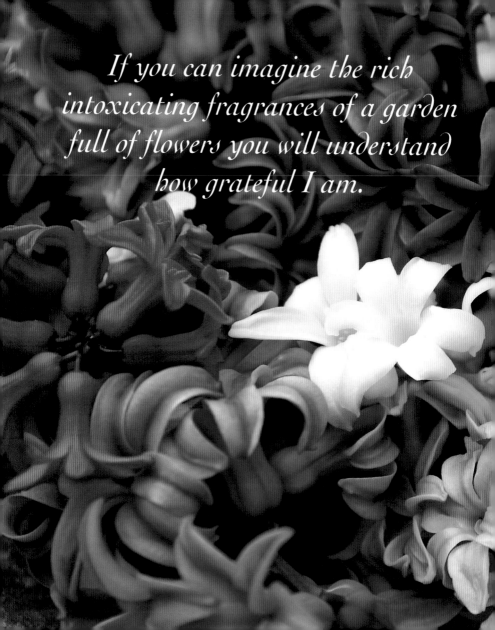

If you can imagine the rich intoxicating fragrances of a garden full of flowers you will understand how grateful I am.

Your quiet and generous support has brought daylight into the shadows of my mind.

Thank You

*Your delicate intrusions
have gently brought me
back to sanity.*

Thank You

Your clear common sense has
brushed away uncertainty.

One day, perhaps I might be able
to return your generosity.

Life springs with new shoots,
thanks to your timely comforts.

*Time is such an effective gift.
You have been so generous
with yours.*

Your kindness and generosity will live with me forever.

Where once I dragged my feet,
now there is a spring in my step,
due, of course, to you.

*Now I can seek peace
in beauty.*

Thank you for helping me to see
the world around as it truly is,
not as I feared it might be.

Just, thank you!

Some gratitude can last a lifetime.

Free at last from the constraints of my heartache, you helped to sustain me through the worst.

Your light has found the
colours I thought had drained
from my life.

*Bold gestures are not necessary,
but often most welcome!*

Even when I felt most exposed,
I knew that you were with me.

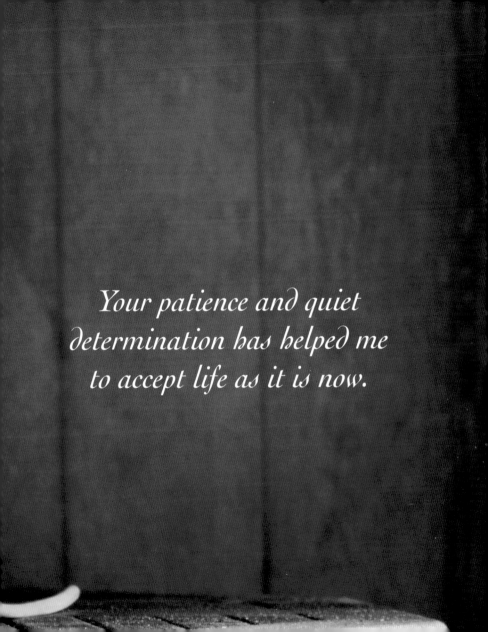

Your patience and quiet determination has helped me to accept life as it is now.

Such expansive generosity one has no right to expect.

Thank You